Praise for *58½ Ways to Improvise in Training*

"This is a fascinating and inspiring book. A must-have for all trainers, teachers, and managers who are looking for innovative ways to enhance creativity, communication, and learning. I recommend Paul Jackson's brilliant book *58½ Ways to Improvise in Training* to all those who want to improve by improvising."

Professor Antonis C Simintiras, PhD, Director of the European Business Management School

"The intriguing title of this book makes one immediately wonder what exactly the half an activity will be. Resisting temptation to flick to the last activity I discovered that Paul Jackson's book was a well-structured, interesting and amusing insight into the professional world of training activities.

"Paul presents a selection of activities that offer ideas to both experienced and novice training presenters. Anyone looking for a swift energising activity to use within his or her training event will find the book invaluable."

Mike Palmer, Professional Training Presenter

"*58½ Ways to Improvise in Training* provides an invaluable collection of innovative activities which would fit any training activity. It contains new ideas for energising and stimulating any age group. The exercises are well grouped enabling you to pick the relevant ones for your event. The simple explanations mean that anyone could pick up and use this resource, and feel confident in their success. I have a wide resource library, so was not expecting to see anything new. I was delighted that this book surprised me!"

Grace Curtin, Management Development Consultant

"As a busy trainer I am always looking for fresh ideas to support learning and change. *58½ Ways to Improvise in Training* offers some great, adaptable activities in a very accessible format, often requiring zero preparation. A very useful resource."

John Hattersley, Inclusive Education Consultant, Cheshire LEA

ing

r

s

Crown House Publishing
www.crownhouse.co.uk

Paperback edition published by

Crown House Publishing Ltd
Crown Buildings, Bancyfelin, Carmarthen, Wales, SA33 5ND, UK
www.crownhouse.co.uk

and

Crown House Publishing Ltd
P.O. Box 2223, Williston, VT 05495-2223, USA
www.CHPUS.com

British Library of Cataloguing-in-Publication Data
A catalogue entry for this book is available
from the British Library.

ISBN 1904424147

LCCN 2003104689

Printed and bound in the UK by
The Cromwell Press Ltd.
Trowbridge, Wiltshire

To my loyal and lovely family

Contents

With thanks to ...

I'd like to thank all those who have generously shared games with me in their workshops. Among those I remember leading workshops are Kit Hollerbach, Lee Simpson, Ian Saville, Chris Salisbury, Murray Edser and George Platts.

George, for example, introduced me to the concept of "New Games", which is well explained in the books *Silver Bullets* and *The New Games Handbook*. Their fascinating history leads us back to conscientious objectors to the Vietnam War.

Some of the theatre-style games can be traced to Keith Johnstone, Augusto Boal, Viola Spolin and doubtless others. Johnstone apart, I haven't had the pleasure of attending their workshops or performances, but their books are all inspirational. And, if their particular ways of running a process have become corrupted in my hands, well that's the way it goes. When you try these activities, they'll probably shift again. As long as you can tweak them into providing satisfactory experiences for your participants and generate whatever work-like metaphors you are seeking, that is fine.

Thanks to Mike and Judy Freeman of Campus Holidays, who gave me a platform to develop some of my first activities and inflict them on willing volunteers some decades ago; and to my fellow executives in the BBC, who first experienced some of these processes during a rather wonderful management training programme.

There are lots of other books of games, many of which I've dipped into (if only to do things differently) and none of which you'll be needing now you've bought this. You have bought it, haven't you?

Away from the activities, I'd like to thank Mark McKergow for his friendship and professional support – plus the fact that he suggested this book in the first place. And a heartfelt thanks to Gower and now Crown House Publishing for their continued support and encouragement.

Foreword

Great teaching is art, and the hallmark of the great artists remains consistent. They are the gifted few who make any subject a joy to learn. In their hands, the driest subject comes sparkling into life and draws you back for more. In his new book, Paul Z Jackson has captured the essence of great teaching artistry for all who want to maximise their effectiveness as educators.

As he did with his bestselling *Impro Learning,* Paul gives us a panoply of immediately usable techniques. Backed by his profound insight, rich philosophy, and practical expertise, those techniques become the tools for instant results in the classroom. In fact, this handbook will serve you equally in a corporate workshop, an extensive training course or a short meeting.

When participant evaluations come back, expect the highest ratings ever. Because, with Paul Z Jackson's help, you will have made learning fun while stimulating creativity, interpersonal communication, engagement in the subject, reflection and self-expression.

Taken at one level, this handbook masterfully prescribes techniques that can be used "as is". Or, if you prefer, the techniques come with suggested variation so you can modify them to suit any teaching situation in which you find yourself. In this way, the handbook serves you as steps of a recipe for success in the classroom.

Taken at another level, this book invites a marvellous transformation within you. The elixir of that transformation comes from the cup of "improvisational energy". Once you catch the buzz of this energy and pass it on to your participants, there is no turning back. You will be hooked and they will, too.

Feel free to use this handbook at whatever level you are ready to accept. Having personally attended the delightful workshops of Paul Z Jackson, I can tell you his techniques work fast to bring you the results you want or need. And having personally transmitted the improvisational energy to participants in my workshops, I know there is no better way to teach.

I heartily encourage you to read and use this handbook. As Paul Z Jackson invites you play, take the bold steps to make these ideas part of your great artistry.

Paul R. Scheele
Chairman, Learning Strategies Corporation
Wayzata, Minnesota, USA
Author of *The PhotoReading Whole Mind System* and *Natural Brilliance*

Introduction

This book is for trainers, facilitators and anyone in need of a swift, energising activity. Each of the activities is improvisational in the sense that it generates what I call *impro energy*, a current that runs between participants. You recognise impro energy when you see people who are clearly "in the moment", alert to whatever is going on in the here and now. It is generally characterised by laughter, prompted by people making things up off the cuff. At its best, impro energy results in *flow*, when the quality of the work is both high and seemingly effortless.

While the activities can be used simply as ice-breakers, they are all amenable to an injection of content. In other words, the facilitator can use them to lead to discussion of various topics – primarily indicated by our chapter titles – because, in doing the activity, the participant will have an experience of that subject.

The book is a companion to my *Impro Learning – How to Make Your Training Creative, Flexible and Spontaneous*, also published in paperback as *The Inspirational Trainer* (Kogan Page).

Where does this stuff come from?

I have engaged in all of these processes with many different people, all of whom have inevitably contributed something. From those rare individuals who point-blank refused to have anything to do with them, I learned how to adapt instructions to make the challenges less daunting.

Such adaptations also catered for most of the "I have a broken leg/dodgy back/weak heart" brigade. Those who maintained they just didn't feel like it often found themselves joining in when they saw how much the participants were enjoying themselves and gaining in relevant experience.

Humour in the trainer's approach creates far more success than threat or excess challenge. It also goes well with an undefensive attitude. There need be nothing at stake if someone doesn't want to play. I recommend, for example, an all-purpose opt-out clause. If there's anything you don't feel like doing, you don't have to do it. We can dignify this further by suggesting that the role of observer may be valuable here.

Yet I invariably assume that everyone *will* take part, and present all the instructions with that expectation confidently in mind. Most of the value is in engaging in these processes. They teach improvisation from the inside. By observing, you'll learn only how to watch improvisation. Perhaps you'll pick up a few tips, too, but then you'll have missed your best chance to practise them.

What do they achieve?

Responses show how the activities work on more than one level. A physical activity warms up limbs, and might also break down barriers between group members. A verbal activity might be an exercise in bonding as well as intellectual dexterity.

Many of the activities are processes in co-creation. Some build skills – often by increasing ways for participants to express themselves. Practitioners will benefit from enhanced creativity, greater flexibility and a boost to their confidence.

Then there is the metaphorical level, whereby the skilled trainer or facilitator never uses the activity merely to put a game into a programme as an ice-breaker or to add variety. The art is to link the activity to the subject of the seminar or workshop. It then serves as a metaphor or illustration of the content. The "Ping-Pong" activity, for example, can be positioned to show how a relaxed attitude to making mistakes often results in fewer errors.

You can uncover many of the metaphorical possibilities of the activities by looking at the questions in the "Debrief" sections. The questions are prompts for generating insights based on the immediate experience, which the facilitator can then link to similar or parallel experiences in the workplace. If you look at the Debrief questions in "A Big Cheese", for example, you will see that they point you towards issues such as assertiveness and taking responsibility.

Visual, verbal and physical triangle

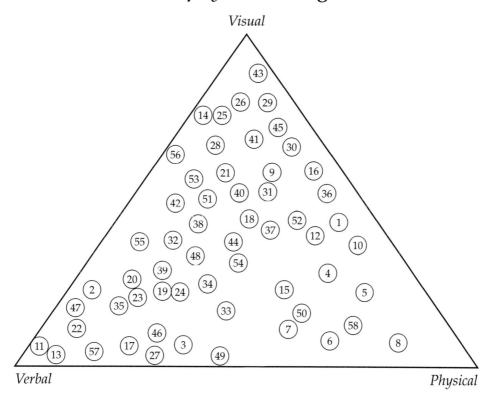

Each activity is plotted between *visual, verbal* and *physical* triangulation points. This will help you choose an activity that has the right mixture of ingredients for example, "Shark Island" under "Alert and Energise" will be more physically demanding than most; "What You Should Have Said" under "Wisdom" is going to be primarily verbal; while "Silent Rooms" under "Scenarios" will balance the visual and physical.

Those in the middle of the triangle will feature a roughly equal balance between verbal, visual and physical elements – a mixture of activities with the variety of visual, verbal and physical involvement you want.

If you have a long talk session in a meeting, you might therefore choose an activity from the other dimensions to re-energise the participants.

Putting into your practice

In running the activities during workshops, I sometimes find the explanation is more complicated than the activity. The faster we start to do it, the faster everyone understands. Here I've made the explanations and instructions as lucid as I can. You may still find that it takes a real running for some of the mechanisms to click into place. If anything remains unclear or if there are variants that you'd like to let me know about, please contact me by email at **paul@impro.org.uk** and I'll do my best to help.

Key to activities

Participants	Time	Energy Level	Individual	Team	Visual	Verbal	Physical
2 - 100	5 Minutes	★ ★ ★ ★ ★	★ ★ ★ ★ ★	★ ★ ★ ★ ★	★ ★ ★ ★ ★	★ ★ ★ ★ ★	★ ★ ★ ★ ★

Ratings for each activity

The ratings as shown in the grid above are measured by:

Participants

The numbers of participants suitable for each activity. This is usually presented as a range within which any number will be comfortable. You might also find ways of working beyond the suggested range.

Time

How long the activity typically takes to complete (scale 0-60 minutes). Nothing in the book need take more than an hour, many can run in about five minutes as energisers.

Energy

How much energy the activity demands of the participants. This ranges from calm to frantic along a five star scale.

Individual/team

A guide to whether the activity is slanted more towards individual learning or team development. The more stars, the more appropriate it is for that sector of development. Most activities in this book develop both the individual and the team.

Visual, verbal and physical

An indicator of how strongly the participants' visual, verbal and physical talents are called upon within the activity. This can be cross-referenced with the Triangle guide on page xi, which also places activities within a visual-verbal-physical frame.

Symbols for each activity

The trainer says

These are word-for-word instructions any trainer or facilitator could use to run the activity. I don't actually recommend using my exact words, because I don't know if they'll fit your style or the precise circumstances of your event.

Still, they are probably the easiest way to gain a sense of how the activity goes.

Bell

You ring the bell to stop the activity – for a new instruction or additional piece of explanation. A harmonious chime is generally more pleasant than a referee's whistle. If you have neither, a handclap will usually suffice.

Sidecoach

With sidecoaching, the activity continues while you give instruction, either to the whole group or to the requisite members. It's the talking (or shouting) you do while the activity is in full swing, and includes encouragement and coaching as well as direct instruction.

Debrief

These are questions to prompt thought and provoke discussion, either partway through or at the end of the active part of the activity. Questions are grouped, and you may find one set of questions more pertinent than another, depending on the outcomes you are after. You may find yourself prompted to ask altogether different questions. It is often a good idea to prepare the questions in advance on a flipchart to reveal at the appropriate moment.

 Variations/developments

Here I list some of the main variations and developments that I have found useful. I suspect all of these activities are responsive to variation. One of the delights of the improvisational approach is the feeling of licence to change whatever seems to need changing. If it isn't working, dispose of it and try something different.

 Equipment

Most of the activities need nothing more than the participants' willingness to give it a go. This section indicates when you need other materials.

Alert and Energise

1. Red, Metal, Organic

Participants	Time	Energy Level	Individual	Team	Visual	Verbal	Physical
2 - 100	5 Minutes	★ ★ ★ ★	★ ★ ★ ★	★	★	★	★ ★ ★ ★

A short warm-up sequence that sensitises people to their surroundings, this gives participants a swift personal experience of the improvisational principle of *here and now*, creating a sense in each person in the room that they are fully present. It works with any number of people and takes very little time.

Trainer says:

"We're going to attune ourselves to what's in the room, here, awakening our senses to our surroundings. It sounds a bit mystical, but it's actually all very practical. On the word 'go', you have thirty seconds to go round the room at your own pace/as fast as you can, touching as many things as you can find that are red. Go."

Bell

"Now find and touch as many things as you can that are made of metal. Thirty seconds. Go."

Bell

"And now as many things as you can find that are organic. [Pause.] That is, which are or were alive."

Debrief

- "Please glance around the room. Does everything red now stand out for you? Metal? Organic?"

- "How did the speed with which you chose to move affect what you found?"

- "Are you slow or speedy? Does it matter?"

- "When we were finding 'organic', did you find it comfortable to touch people? Did you mind people touching you?"

- "How is this quality of *here and now* going to help you during the day/during your work?"

Variations/developments

While the exercise is usually run in a room, it works equally effectively outside – almost as a miniature treasure hunt. Following that train of thought, you could easily develop it into a more elaborate game by asking participants to find a selection of more and less obvious items.

You could also explore questions of achievement, frustration or appreciation of surroundings and one's relationship to them while in a state of *here and now*.

One improvisational aspect for the trainer is to vary what you ask them to touch or find. You can create sudden shifts and surges in energy by repeating categories and switching fast between them.

2. Name and Back One

Participants	Time	Energy Level	Individual	Team	Visual	Verbal	Physical
2 - 100	5 Minutes	★ ★	★ ★ ★ ★ ★		★	★ ★ ★ ★	★

This gets everyone through the sometimes awkward barrier of speaking aloud in the group. Everyone starts to say words they may not have been expecting to say – exercising the improvisational qualities of immediacy and surprise. It attunes us to our first thoughts, which are often the most useful.

As this activity continues the theme of alertness, it forms a natural follow-on to "Red, Metal, Organic".

It is a good game for multicultural groups, as everyone can use their own language.

Trainer says:

"On the word 'go', you have one minute to go round the room touching – or pointing at – and naming as many different items as you can find: for example, 'chair', 'ceiling', 'window latch'."

Debrief

If no one else mentions it, the trainer can express how amazing it is that there are so many different objects in what had perhaps previously seemed a rather bland and ordinary room. A good metaphor, perhaps, for some of the learnings that will be emerging later during the event.

Trainer says:

"Now, for a mental shake-up, point at items in the room, naming the item you were previously pointing at." (The trainer demonstrates, if possible.)

Bell

"If you find yourself getting stuck, stop and start again. This is a good example of the improvisational principle of *disposability*. If it doesn't work, chuck it out and begin afresh."

Bell

"Let's stop before anyone's brain gets permanently scrambled."

Debrief

- "How easy was that?"

- "What makes it difficult?"

- "Beyond that, what do you add yourself to make it even harder?"

- "What were you doing – or not doing – at the times when it flowed for you?"

The trainer can add:

"This is a good mental exercise that you can practise out on the streets. Obviously, try not to be too flamboyant!"

3. Ping-Pong

Participants	Time	Energy Level	Individual	Team	Visual	Verbal	Physical
2 - 100	15 Minutes	★ ★ ★ ★	★ ★	★ ★ ★		★ ★ ★	★ ★

This is a communication game, in which partners succeed by establishing a rhythm together. The temptation is to try to catch your partner out, which can also be fun. There's often a lot of laughter.

It is a game for pairs or for a sequence of pairs. Games for a sequence of pairs are something of a rarity. Depending on how many pairings you want everyone to experience, you can call "Change partners" more – or less – frequently.

Trainer says:

"Find a partner. This is a fast-moving game, so it's not a commitment for life – though it can be if you want it to be, of course. Actually, you'll be changing partners very soon, and can notice the differences between one partner and the next.

"One of you is A, the other is B: it doesn't matter which is which. We're going to play Ping-Pong, and A is going to serve first. A serves a 'Ping', to which B responds with a 'Pong'."

Trainer demonstrates that "Ping" and "Pong" are purely verbal, played with partners face to face, preferably standing.

Trainer continues:

"It's a game of rhythm, A serves one 'Ping' at a time, waits for the 'Pong', then serves another 'Ping' and so on. Find what rhythm suits you and your partner best, then vary it."

After about 25 seconds, the trainer says:

"Change server. B is 'Ping' and A is 'Pong'."

The trainer needs to remember to call "Change server" every half-minute or so throughout the sequence, until he or she judges the moment is right to hand the responsibility over to the group, saying, "You decide with your partner when you want to change server."

After A has served two sequences of "pings", the trainer says:

"Change partner."

New partners play the same game for a minute or two.

Bell

Now A can serve either a "ping" or a "pong". If A serves a "Ping", B responds with a "Pong". If A serves a "Pong", B responds with a "Ping". A can serve any sequence of "Pings" or "Pongs" – but only one of anything until B responds. It's still a game of rhythm.

Sidecoach

Trainer circulates, encouraging players to vary speed.

Debrief

- "How did your partners vary?"

- "How did the difference in partners make a difference in you?"

- "Were some pairings you experienced more cooperative and others more competitive?"

- "Any parallels to work life there? Or home life?"

- "How did you react to mistakes? Were you annoyed with yourself, cross with your partner, or was there a smattering of healthy laughter?"

Impro note

One improvisational element here for the trainer is to judge the moments to swap servers, swap partners and keep the game moving. The simplicity makes it very easy to learn and play, but also brings a danger of boredom as the learning points are recognised and there's no further novelty (by way of a new partner, or a new variation to the game).

Improvisational elements for the participants include the experience of making instant choices – of partner and of the sequence they elect to serve up. It illustrates the impro principle of freedom within structure in a very simple way. The structure at its most basic is the choice each server makes between Ping and Pong, with the freedom to choose one or the other. It's amazing how some players get themselves tangled even within such a simple improvisational framework.

Variations/developments

Allow the server to serve three "balls" at once, of any combination of Pings and Pongs, to which the receiver responds with the converse: e.g. "pong, pong, ping" – "ping, ping, pong".

4. Scream Circle

Participants	Time	Energy Level	Individual	Team	Visual	Verbal	Physical
10 - 80	5 Minutes	★ ★ ★ ★ ★	★	★ ★ ★ ★	★	★	★ ★ ★ ★

A chance for a blast of noise and fast energy. In my experience, "Scream Circle" has worked better with younger and less inhibited groups, but can work well with variants for a more reserved bunch. It can also turn a reserved bunch into an uninhibited group – if the trainer presents it and demonstrates with sufficient confidence.

Trainer says:

"Everyone form a circle, giving yourself a shoulder width of room to the next person. Everyone tilt your head towards the floor and close your eyes. Together we count aloud to three, and on three we all look up and – if you make eye contact with anyone – you scream and change places with them by running across the circle."

Sidecoach

"Who hasn't made eye contact with anyone yet? Why not? What's it going to take?"

Debrief

• "Who wasn't quite sure whether or not they'd made eye contact sometimes?"

• "How can that be clearer, and what does that tell us about communication, and clarity in communication?"

11

Variations/developments

The trainer sets a target of how many times each player should cross the circle – say three crosses, each with a different partner.

The improvisational element is largely in the alertness quality of *here and now*, which is required in order to succeed in the mutual catching of eyes. It's also there in the clearer nonverbal communications that result when players improve their performance in the light of the debriefing questions.

You can build in a greater awareness of physicality by adding rules, such as, "No one is to touch anyone else as you run across the circle" or, "Every time you cross the circle you must lightly make contact with the person you are crossing with."

5. Target Bluff

Participants	Time	Energy Level	Individual	Team	Visual	Verbal	Physical
4 - 10	5 Minutes	★ ★ ★	★	★ ★ ★ ★	★	★	★ ★ ★ ★

This is an exercise in physical and mental dexterity, in which the group work improves as individuals master the skills involved.

Trainer says:

"We'll warm up by simply throwing the ball gently and underarm to each other to catch. Throw to anyone you like."

Use a koosh ball or softball, nothing harder than a tennis ball unless it's a really macho gang.

Bell

Now point at one person as you throw the ball to someone else.

Sidecoach

"How many variants are there? Which hand throws and which hand does the pointing? Are you always throwing to the same person? Or pointing at the same person?"

Debrief

- "How much flexibility were you able to achieve?"

- "Did it matter if people chose you or neglected you?"

Impro note

This is a simple structure with a pleasing degree of freedom. There's always enough choice of whom to throw to, with a selection of accompanying pointing movements to choose, to keep the variety going with a modicum of physical challenge. (Will my limbs behave with the elegance I desire?)

This was a regular warm-up favourite of one of my improvisational comedy groups. Half a dozen of them would play it for about five minutes before every show.

6. Shark Island

Participants	Time	Energy Level	Individual	Team	Visual	Verbal	Physical
10 - 100	5 Minutes	★ ★ ★ ★ ★		★ ★ ★ ★ ★		★	★ ★ ★ ★

A good warm-up if you propose to work with groups and subgroups. Also fast and physical.

Individuals swap from group to group quickly, for no particular personal reasons, forming and disbanding alliances as they go.

Trainer says:

"You're all on the sea, and the sea is infested with sharks. The only way to gain safety is to form an island. An island consists of a group of people containing a certain number. I shall shout out the safe number – which will keep changing.

"Anyone who doesn't get into a group of the right size will be consumed by the sharks, and is required to perform a spectacular and noisy death.

"Three. Eight. Seventeen. Two …" (And so forth.)

Debrief

- "How did you feel when you were part of a safe group?"

- "How did you feel when you were left out or failed to get in?"

- "How did you feel when you were thrown to the sharks – when a group reduced by one, for example)?"

- "How dramatic were you able to make your death?"

Variations/developments

Each time a number is repeated, participants must form a group with different people from the last time that number came up.

Play a quieter and less dramatic version by leaving out the death-playing aspect.

Play a more physically demanding version by dividing the area into halves or quadrants and randomly varying the areas in which safe islands may be formed.

7. Fast Lines

Participants	Time	Energy Level	Individual	Team	Visual	Verbal	Physical
6 - 100	5 Minutes	★ ★ ★	★ ★	★ ★ ★	★	★ ★	★ ★ ★

This involves quick sorting into a series of lines, ranked by various criteria. It makes people move and begin to see themselves in relation to the others in the group against those criteria. It can also demonstrate the power of knowledge and repetition in learning, and serve as a metaphor, for example, for databasing.

Trainer says:

"On the word 'go', arrange yourself in a line in order of height. Go.

"Now in order of shoe size.

"Now in order of birth date, ignoring the year of birth: i.e. January, February and so forth."

Variations/developments

Use other criteria – whatever you like: perhaps including hair-length, length of service with the organisation, number of cousins, size of iris. It depends on how much revelation and intimacy you want at this stage.

Repeat some of the categories and time how long it takes on the subsequent occasions, either by stopwatch or group impression. The repetition can be either during the same playing of the exercise, or – perhaps more interestingly – a day or more later.

Debrief

- "Any surprises?"

- "How much does movement help you to find out this information?"

- "How much does it help you remember the information?"

Working Together

8. Beach World Support

Participants	Time	Energy Level	Individual	Team	Visual	Verbal	Physical
6 - 100	15 Minutes	★ ★ ★		★ ★ ★ ★ ★		★	★ ★ ★ ★

A physical warm-up and a mild intellectual challenge for a group or for a number of teams.

Needs between three and eight players per team.

Trainer says:

"Each team has a beach ball, which they must carry through the obstacle course – or from one end of the room to another. Each player can have only one finger on the ball at any one time, and all fingers must be below the middle axis of the ball.

"One of the trickiest parts is to get the ball up and supported in the first instance. So we'll divide the race into two parts. The first part is to find the quickest team to get the ball up into a starting position.

"As teams are ready to begin, they can practise manipulating the ball, lifting and lowering, and moving at various speeds.

"When the race begins, if a ball is dropped or the umpire – me – sees anyone breaking the rules using more than one finger per person or a finger over the horizon, that team goes back and starts again."

There's often a fair bit of deliberate or inadvertent cheating, so be strict and get as many teams to go back and restart as you can.

Debrief

• "How did your team organise itself?"

- "How did you deal with the frustrations and difficulties that the task presented?"

- "Was there a leader, and how was the role allocated? If there was no leader, how did you each know what to do?"

 Equipment

Beach-balls or tennis-balls.

9. Copycats

Participants	Time	Energy Level	Individual	Team	Visual	Verbal	Physical
5 - 15	5 Minutes	★ ★	★ ★	★ ★ ★	★ ★ ★	★ ★ ★	★ ★ ★

A great opening-of-session process for an active group, to explore and extend their levels of energy, creativity and trust.

Decide how long you want the warming-up to last, then divide the time between the number of participants.

Impro note

This is a game to return to a number of times with the same group. On first playing, about thirty seconds to one minute is probably long enough. With a good group on return visits, you needn't set a time limit at all, and wondrous scenes can spontaneously develop. The freedom to choose how long to lead for and how much to do leads to great confidence, which is redoubled when players see everyone else echoing their movements.

 Trainer says:

"In the Copycat warm-up, we're each going to lead the activity for thirty seconds, then pass to the next person you care to point at.

"When you're leading, everyone else in the group will mirror what you do (or obey your directions, if it's something that needs explaining).

"You can do whatever you like – and the rest of us will follow."

Sidecoach

"Pass on to the next leader, please."

It's important for the facilitator to keep a vigilant sense of how long each person's turn should last, to encourage the timid to keep going a few moments longer, or to get the enthusiast to pass on when their point has been made.

Variations/developments

The group as a whole are obliged to cover a range of activity between them. For example, we want physical, facial and vocal warm ups in the next five minutes.

Whoever carries on must use the finishing position of the previous leader. This variant turns the process into an illustration and practice of the impro principle of *Yes ... And*. You have to accept the offering and build on it, even if you had something different in mind.

With many groups, the first run of "Copycats" is pretty tame, as people confine themselves to stock stretches from gym class or yoga. When they gain confidence that everyone will indeed copy them, the urge to lead with a touch of flair, imagination and improvisation can be most impressive.

Debrief

Usually best left silent, to allow the group to appreciate their imagination (or lack of it), and to get on with the next process.

10. Shapelines

Participants	Time	Energy Level	Individual	Team	Visual	Verbal	Physical
8 - 80	15 Minutes	★ ★ ★ ★ ★		★ ★ ★ ★ ★	★		★ ★ ★ ★

This is one of the most physically demanding processes in the repertoire. It gets participants stretching and moving and working hard, yet it is self-regulated, so those who prefer to take it down a notch are able to do so.

This works well to bond a group, to develop individuals' senses of precision of movement, harmony with colleagues and rhythm of a physical task.

Trainer says:

"Form into lines of four. One person behind another. Each line parallel to the others, to start with. The person at the front of the line make a shape – any shape. You don't have to make the same shape as the person at the front of another line. Each group improvises differently within the same structure.

"People at the front of the lines, hold your shape steady. Now, the person at the back of the line comes to the front and copies the exact same shape of the person who was first at the front.

"Again, the person at the back of the line comes to the front and copies the exact same shape of the person who was first at the front. And again."

At this point, each line should have four people in the same shape as each other.

"Now the person at the back – the original leader – comes to the front again, and makes a new shape. It can be completely contrasting or something slightly different. It's entirely up to you.

"And, as before, the person at the back of the line comes to the front and copies the exact same shape of the person who was first at the front. And again.

"If your line is about to bump into a wall, a table or another line, be aware of your surroundings and, as you come to the front, adjust the direction your shapeline is heading in."

Impro note

This game often involves plenty of improvisational sidecoaching for the trainer. Sidecoach tightly for the first few rounds of "Shapelines", since it can be a little tricky for some people to grasp. Once they get the idea, and relax into it, it becomes far more automatic, and your sidecoaching can concentrate on encouraging:

- the person at the back to make a swift move to the front;

- greater precision in the copying of the previous person's shape.

 Bell

Pause the activity.

 Trainer says:

"The next part gives everyone the chance to be the leader. Person at the front of each line make a shape. Person at the back come to the front, make the same shape – *and now change it by one movement of one limb.*

"Person at the back, come to the front, and adopt the shape of your predecessor, and change it by one movement of one limb. And again from the person at the back. Keep it moving and precise and flowing. We should see the shape gradually change as we look along the line."

Debrief

- "How precise were you able to be in your copying?"

- "How inventive was your group?"

- "Did you notice what the other groups were doing?"

- "Did you enjoy leading?"

- "Did you prefer following?"

- "How conscious were your moves?"

- "Did you get into the 'flow' and find things easier?"

11. One Word

Participants	Time	Energy Level	Individual	Team	Visual	Verbal	Physical
3 - 12	5 Minutes	★	★	★ ★ ★		★ ★ ★ ★ ★	

A classic from improvisational theatre, which prompts plenty of laughter on most occasions. This is a strongly verbal game, and can prove tricky in English for non-native English speakers.

Trainer says:

"We're going to form a circle, and tell a story one word each at a time. When you say a word, you point to the person who's going to say the next word in the story.

"At the end of each sentence, we don't need to say the punctuation marks. Just start the next sentence, as you would do in normal speech."

Sidecoach

If the story breaks down, or the grammar gets too convoluted, chuck the story away and start a new one. In improvisation, everything is disposable. There's always another one coming along.

Allow only one word from each person a time.

Recognise the end of a story and allow it to finish.

Debrief

• "Who created the story? Who was the leader?"

• "What responsibility does each person have for each other?"

- "What responsibility does each person have for the story?"

- "How does the speed with which you contribute the next word affect the quality of the output?"

Impro note

One-word stories teach many improvisational skills, including the spontaneity needed to keep up the pace of the story, flexibility – when you have to follow a word you were not expecting – and creativity.

12. Happiness Machines

Participants	Time	Energy Level	Individual	Team	Visual	Verbal	Physical
8 - 100	20 Minutes	★ ★		★ ★ ★ ★ ★	★ ★	★ ★	★ ★ ★ ★

Small groups each create a series of machines in which the participants are all the working parts. Some groups spend their time discussing how they'll do it. Others simply work it out by doing it. The latter are usually more successful.

Trainer says:

"A machine requires that each part touch at least one other part at least some of the time. In your groups, you have five minutes to devise a sausage-making machine, which you'll present to the other groups."

Bell

"Each group takes a turn to present their machine.

"Now, in the same groups, make a machine that makes some kind of weather.

"And now a machine that makes happiness.

"Finally, a machine that builds itself and takes itself apart again: a self-build, self-destroy machine."

Variations/developments

Any sequence from physical product (sausage, hats, shoes) to less machine-likely products (sunshine, rain, tennis serve) to abstract product. Such sequencing encourages increasing creativity and imagination, and stretches the group further into improvisational territory.

Debrief

- "Which machines that you have just seen did you admire the most, and why?"

- "What made those machines successful?"

- "What was the best balance between discussing it and trying it?"

- "Could you work together on this activity entirely without talking?"

13. A Big Cheese

Participants	Time	Energy Level	Individual	Team	Visual	Verbal	Physical
3 - 12	10 Minutes	★	★ ★	★ ★ ★		★ ★ ★ ★ ★	

"A Big Cheese" is also known as "The Alphabet Game". Can you work out why?

The activity offers a huge amount of variety within the very familiar structures of "story" and the alphabet. This can be run as a quietly creative process, with the group sitting on chairs, or as a more energised process with dramatic flourishes encouraged.

Trainer says:

"We're going to tell a story in which each sentence starts with successive letters of the alphabet. Each of you in turn gives us one sentence of the story. No more, no fewer. Let's start with 'A' and go through to 'Z'. The story can be about anything at all.

"As I left my house this morning, I noticed a strange glow on the horizon."

Sidecoach

Say the first thought.

Encourage cheating if the story gets stuck on "x": "Excellent results can be had in this way."

Debrief

• "Given the instructions, what could you do to improve the quality of the output – that is, tell a better story between you?"

- "How much of the struggle was really to do with remembering the next letter in the alphabet, and how much with taking a decision about what you were prepared to say?"

Variations/developments

- Start with different letters of the alphabet.

- Make it easier by listing the letters on flipchart.

- Make it harder by banning dialogue within the story.

- Make it more rigorous and immediate by telling a story only in the present tense.

Alphabet scene. Two or more participants create an improvised scene or playlet, in which they alternate lines of dialogue, each starting with successive letters of the alphabet. This is much harder than an alphabet story, as they have to look after their dramatic relationship and the physical actions, and still keep an ear on the progression of the letters. When it's good, it's very good, but for advanced practitioners – or extreme experimenters – only.

14. Team Pix

Participants	Time	Energy Level	Individual	Team	Visual	Verbal	Physical
5 - 12	60 Minutes	★ ★		★ ★ ★ ★ ★	★ ★ ★ ★	★	

This is an enjoyable activity in which the group take photographs of themselves. The task involves planning, doing, sorting and presenting. Each phase invites a debriefing on how closely the way the group perceives itself matches the actual way its members work together.

Trainer says:

"You have one hour in which to plan, take and present ten photographs. These must illustrate what you want to show about the way your team works together.

"They don't have to be literal pictures of you doing your usual work – though you can include this if you wish. Use your imaginations, to show metaphors or images of the way you are as a team. Highlight individual and group strengths and qualities."

Debrief

Discuss the images and captions.

"Did the way you worked together to complete the task reflect the images you chose to present in your pictures?"

This is an interesting example of a layer within a layer. It should be apparent to what extent the group has "walked its talk". I have seen one instance where a dictatorial leader composed a series of photographs intended to illustrate what a democratic unit the group was.

Variations/developments

You can vary the length of time and number of pictures required, depending on the size of the group and the degree of time pressure you wish them to experience.

Increase the quality you require in the display – proper mountings, neat captions.

Equipment

• Camera: Polaroid or electronic are best for instant pictures. With traditional photography you'll need to consider the time required for developing film. This can be incorporated as an additional challenge for the group.

• Display board.

• Mountings.

• Marker pens.

Influencing Relationships

15. What Are You Doing?

Participants	Time	Energy Level	Individual	Team	Visual	Verbal	Physical
5 - 40	5 Minutes	★ ★	★ ★ ★	★ ★	★ ★	★ ★	★ ★ ★ ★

Played in a circle, this is a game of influence – and revenge. An activity for any number as the elements of drama and surprise make it watchable while you wait your turn.

Trainer says:

"The first person in the circle (a volunteer or perhaps the trainer) mimes a simple everyday activity, such as brushing hair or writing a letter. The next person in the circle asks, 'What are you doing?' *While continuing to perform the mime*, the person replies, 'I'm …' and names an activity that can be anything except the one they are actually performing. So they might say, 'I'm riding a horse.'

"When they've named the new activity, the person who asked the question has to mime the new activity – in this instance riding a horse. They, in turn, are asked by the next person in the circle, 'What are you doing?'

"As the activity passes round the circle, each person has to nominate a new activity for their neighbour to perform. No repeats. When the person next to you starts their mime, you stop yours."

Bell

When the circle has completed the task once or twice round.

Trainer says:

"Now's your chance for revenge. This time we'll go round anticlockwise, so you'll be setting the activity for the person who was previously setting it for you."

Sidecoach

You may need to remind beginners to carry on the activity while nominating the next one. That is the moment of maximum improvisation, when either the physical action or the mental task of naming a new activity has to be carried out spontaneously – without conscious thought. The one provides sufficient distraction for the other, which is an interesting state to reflect upon.

Debrief

- "What was the feeling while you named a new activity while performing the old one?"

- "Were you able to play spontaneously – that is, not decide in advance what you would be saying?"

Variations/developments

"What are you doing?" Challenge.

Invite two volunteers to step into the middle of the circle and compete until one fails to perform the mime or answer the question with a new answer. As any contender loses, a new challenger steps in to take the place. This is a competitive variant, with winners, losers and all that implies. Played quick-fire, it can be an exciting spectacle with plenty of invention, and it visibly sharpens the improvisational capabilities as players find the balance between thought and action.

16. Silent Focus

Participants	Time	Energy Level	Individual	Team	Visual	Verbal	Physical
5 - 15	10 Minutes	★ ★	★	★ ★ ★ ★	★ ★ ★		★ ★ ★

This is a classic, simple activity that serves as a practice in giving and taking. It's also an excellent metaphor for any give-and-take situation that a facilitator or trainer may want to illuminate.

Trainer says:

"Only one person is allowed to move at any one time. And, at any one time, one person must be moving. It is the group's responsibility to achieve this.

"While one person moves, they can make any movement they wish. I recommend that you make it a continuous movement, as it's harder for others to work with a stop-start, jerky movement. That person keeps the movement going until someone else starts a new movement. When you start a new movement, it is called *taking focus* – and at that precise moment the first mover stops."

Sidecoach

•   Keep your movement going until somebody else takes focus. You don't give focus until someone else takes it.

•   This is essentially a silent game.

•   What do you need to do to give people who haven't yet taken focus the chance to do so?

Debrief

- "How well did the group succeed in its task?"

- "Was there a good sharing of responsibility?"

- "What did you, individually, contribute? Was it easier for you to give focus or to take focus?"

- "How could you improve giving and taking of focus in the game?"

- "How could you improve giving and taking of focus in the work setting?"

- "How can you be more assertive in the taking of responsibility?"

- "How can you be more freely creative during the moments when you have the focus?"

- "What connection can you make between taking focus in this activity and adding value in the workplace?"

Variations/developments

In the simplest version, everyone starts in a circle or wherever they happen to be in the room. In the variation, try starting with people facing away from each other, or in awkward corners.

17. Noisy Focus

Participants	Time	Energy Level	Individual	Team	Visual	Verbal	Physical
5 - 15	10 Minutes	★ ★	★	★ ★ ★ ★		★	★ ★ ★ ★

This is the companion piece to "Silent Focus", and can be run immediately afterwards to develop the theme, or as a contrasting activity later during a programme.

Note also the "Focus Complete" activity, which combines "Silent Focus" and "Noisy Focus" into a more complex activity for those who are familiar with the two basic activities.

Trainer says:

"Everyone stands back to back in a circle. One person makes a noise and sustains the noise until another person 'takes focus' by starting a new noise (which they then continue). When focus is taken from you, become silent again, until you want to take focus again, either with the same noise you used before or a new one."

Sidecoach

- Noises can be made by parts of the body other than the mouth.

- Make sure you can – and do – sustain the noise until someone takes focus.

Debrief

Same as for "Silent Focus".

Variations/developments

Everyone lies on their back in a circle with their head towards the centre, feet towards the circumference.

18. Focus Complete

Participants	Time	Energy Level	Individual	Team	Visual	Verbal	Physical
5 - 15	10 Minutes	★ ★ ★ ★	★	★ ★ ★ ★	★ ★ ★	★ ★ ★	★ ★

This is a combination of "Silent Focus" and "Noisy Focus", in which participants take focus each time either with a sound or with a movement (but not – and this is the tricky discipline – both). The art is to find minimal ways of taking focus. How subtle – and yet definite – can the give and take be between members of the group?

Trainer says:

"Now let's combine 'Silent Focus' and 'Noisy Focus'. Start where you like in the space, and you can either make a noise, or a movement, but not both at the same time. Someone else takes focus by making a noise or a move that catches your attention. Vary the ways in which you take focus – and find which are the subtlest."

Sidecoach

The sidecoaching in "Focus Complete" is usually to:

• remind participants to be as subtle as possible;

• restart the activity when focus breaks down completely because either no one or more than one person appears to have taken it;

• help the group out of the difficulties of the extremes by asking, for example, "If you are facing away from everyone, are you more likely to be successful taking focus by a movement or a sound?"; "A quiet sound or a noisy one?" and so on.

19. Madrigal

Participants	Time	Energy Level	Individual	Team	Visual	Verbal	Physical
5 - 15	15 Minutes	★ ★	★	★ ★ ★ ★	★	★ ★ ★ ★	★

A chance for participants to use their own voices to express themselves, then listen and combine voices with others. Yet this is far simpler and less taxing than singing (which is great for those with any kind of fear or nervousness about singing).

Each madrigal is performed by a line of people, guided by a conductor. The conductor is usually the facilitator, though after some practice the role may be passed to participants.

The more in the line, the greater the potential complications. With a group of fifteen, I would have three consecutive lines of five, perhaps having a couple of turns each, taking approximately thirty minutes in total. A good conductor can manage a couple of dozen participants in one session.

 Trainer says:

"Each person in turn needs a 'line' for their part in 'Madrigal'. A 'line' is a series of words, between four and eight words long. To get your line, you can either make one up yourself or ask the audience (or colleagues or whoever).

"You could, for example, ask for a well-known phrase or saying, and find yourself given the line, 'A stitch in time saves nine' or 'Many hands make light work'.

"When everyone has got their line, the conductor indicates that one person is to start repeating their line. They can speak, chant or sing – it doesn't matter as long as its rhythmic.

"The conductor has a set of signals:

- **Pointing**: Indicates to which performers the signals will apply

- **Motioning**: The performers join in

- **Hand slash**: The performers stop

- **Hand raised**: Increase volume

- **Hand lowered**: Decrease volume

"The conductor is also entitled to negotiate or improvise any other signals, as they feel fit.

"While the first participant continues, the conductor brings in another performer with their line, which the performer should match to the rhythm and tempo of the first performer.

"Gradually the conductor engages each participant into the madrigal, using the signals to create as harmonious and interesting a set of sounds as possible.

"Once the basic madrigal is established, the performers begin to improvise by replacing one or two of the words from their original line with one or two of the words they are hearing from a nearby performer. So our two exemplars could now be chanting, "A stitch in time saves light' and 'Many stitches make light work'.

"As the madrigal continues, the performers make more intricate variations, and the conductor creates solos for the enjoyment of performers and audience."

Debrief

- "How were you able to keep your own performance going, and also incorporate the input of others?"

- "What was the balance of creativity between conductor and performer?"

- "How can you listen while you are at the same time making a noise?"

- "Is this a skill you might develop for work circumstances?"

- For those wary of singing: "Did anyone find themselves in danger of singing?"

20. Finish the ...

Participants	Time	Energy Level	Individual	Team	Visual	Verbal	Physical
4 - 100	5 Minutes	★	★ ★ ★ ★	★	★	★ ★ ★ ★	

The idea is simple. Two participants take it in turns to complete each other's sentences. This is an amusing and advanced-communications game. It's advanced because, when played poorly, it is frustrating for participants and spectators alike – and where's the fun in that? When participants play it really well, they face another danger – that of resembling an old married couple.

Trainer says:

"Each pair is going to tell a story. You tell it between you, one sentence each at a time, with the last word of the sentence missing. Your partner completes the sentence, then says all but the last word of the next sentence."

Variations/developments

Either each pair performs simultaneously, or pairs take it in turns to perform for the rest of the group. In playing to the rest of the group, a good variant is for them to give a lecture. You can guarantee the improvisational nature of the lecture by having the audience decide the topic immediately before the lecture is delivered.

Have one partner provide all the information, except the last word of each sentence; and the partner is purely the sentence finisher.

Debrief

• "Were you stronger at starting sentences, or ending them?"

- "What choices was your partner making that helped or hindered your efforts?"

- "Under what conditions can you and a partner reach a state of near-telepathy?"

21. Dubbing

Participants	Time	Energy Level	Individual	Team	Visual	Verbal	Physical
4 - 16	25 Minutes	★ ★	★ ★ ★	★ ★	★ ★ ★	★ ★	★

One participant provides the speech, while another performs the physical actions that match the speech. In this way, two participants (or pairs of participants) build a base of cooperation from which they can launch excursions of influence.

Trainer says:

"In this pair, one of you is A, the other B. You act as one, with A on the side, providing the voice, and B in the middle, providing the actions. You are going to demonstrate how to make something, which will be suggested by the audience."

Sidecoach

Ask the audience to provide a subject for the dubbing pair to demonstrate.

Encourage the dubbers to take their time: they need to be alert and responsive to each other to create the illusion of telepathy or working with one mind.

Development

Once you have established how the game works and some participants have succeeded in dubbing an activity, bring two pairs into play, having a dialogue with each other. A speaks for B, while C speaks for D. Ask the audience for a location where a pair of characters might meet, or for a task that it takes two people to accomplish.

Debrief

- "Have you ever had to act out another's bidding?"

- "How can that person make things easier for you – or more difficult?"

- "How much cooperation do you need, before you start exerting your influence?"

- "Does the speaker influence the mover, or vice versa?"

- "How can you allow yourself to be influencer as well as influenced?"

- "What are the benefits if you both influence each other?"

Development

A particularly tricky and impressive feat is for A to speak for B, B for C and C for A. Worth trying if the improvisational energy is flowing well and three participants really relish a challenge. Advise them to start their scene as simply as possible – entering the action one at a time – and to create bold, distinctive characters.

Impro note

For the activity to succeed, it requires the players to demonstrate the improvisational quality of Yes ... And – that is, accepting and building – within the pairings and between the pairings. And to keep Yes ... And-ing to allow the scene or task to develop.

Resources

22. Pocket Piece

Participants	Time	Energy Level	Individual	Team	Visual	Verbal	Physical
2 - 100	10 Minutes	★	★ ★ ★ ★ ★		★	★ ★ ★ ★	

A simple, works-anywhere way of getting people to start communicating with each other on the basis of their own personal preferences and resources.

Trainer says:

"Everybody find a partner. Now select an item from your pocket or your bag (or, if we're being really formal, your briefcase) and tell your partner about it. When you've finished, your partner reveals all about their item.

Sidecoach

•   "Tell your partner the personal significance of the item."

•   "What story do you associate with the item?"

•   "Why did you choose that one, rather than something else you have with you?"

•   "What could the item say about you if it could speak?"

Variations/developments

Each person speaks to the whole group about their selected item.

Each pair reports back something to the group that they have discovered about their partners.

23. Name That Name

Participants	Time	Energy Level	Individual	Team	Visual	Verbal	Physical
3 - 20	10 Minutes	★	★ ★ ★ ★ ★			★ ★ ★ ★ ★	

A relatively intimate and quiet way of starting a group session. A good one to use if you think the participants will readily open up to each other, or if you want to give them that opportunity – and are ready to deal with consequences whether they do or don't.

Trainer says:

"We're going to introduce ourselves to the group in turn. First say your name, then tell us what you feel about your name or what you think about your name."

Development

Ask each person what they would like to be known as during the event. They may choose a version of their name – Bob rather than Robert, for instance – and just occasionally someone requests that we call them a completely new name or a name they have not used for ages.

Debrief

* "How free did you feel about revealing yourself?"

* "Did you choose to tell us what you feel or what you think?"

* "There's a theory that women are more comfortable speaking of feelings and men of thoughts – I wonder if this group's experience in this introduction bears that out."

- "Does it matter what name we call someone?"

- "What does this tell us for client or customer relationships?"

24. Category Cruncher

Participants	Time	Energy Level	Individual	Team	Visual	Verbal	Physical
8 - 80	10 Minutes	★ ★	★ ★	★ ★ ★	★ ★	★ ★ ★ ★	★ ★

A quick-fire energiser, which also introduces the idea of resources by inviting participants to consider which categories – resourceful or otherwise – they fit. They also find out various things they have in common or difference with each other. And, in the prototype negotiations, they make fast decisions, enjoying the improvisational activity of choosing freely within a series of shifting structures.

Trainer says:

"In this activity you need to find things out about each other quickly and sort yourselves into groups.

"Each group is identified by what you have in common regarding the category that I call out.

"Let's try it – the category is pets."

Sidecoach

The participants might split into just two groups – those with pets and those without. If there are more than ten participants, encourage them to find further or different ways of splitting; for example, dog owners, cat owners, used to have a pet, never had a pet.

Trainer says:

"A group means at least two people, so no one is to be left on their own. For example, if the category is weddings, and everyone has had one except for

63

one person, that cannot be the basis of the groups. You might need to find a group who have been to weddings this year, and a group who haven't."

Other categories to call out might include:

- siblings

- marital status

- transport

- education

As the categories get more interesting, so the participants may take longer to identify which group is which, and to choose which group they are in (often they will qualify for more than one within any category – for example, in transport someone may own a bike, a car and a yacht).

Debrief

- "What have you found out that you didn't know before – about the others?"

- "What about yourself?"

- "How did you decide what to do when you had a choice within a category?"

- "How did you feel about breaking up the groups so quickly?"

- "Were there some people you were inclined to stick with no matter what the category?"

25. Achievement Gallery

Participants	Time	Energy Level	Individual	Team	Visual	Verbal	Physical
3 - 12	30 Minutes	★	★ ★ ★ ★	★	★ ★ ★ ★ ★	★	

A quiet and intensive way of discovering and revealing resources. It begins with participants working individually, then they share their achievements.

Trainer says:

"Each take a sheet of paper and drawing materials. On your own, draw a picture of the achievement of which you feel most proud. There are no prizes for drawing – matchstick figures are perfectly acceptable.

"Your achievement can be from any time in your life. It may be from home, work, a hobby, academic or social. Whatever makes you most proud. It can be something you achieved in a particular instant, or that took a period of time."

Bell

"Now write on the borders of your picture all the personal qualities you needed to make that achievement.

"Don't be modest. Imagine someone asking, 'What did this person need to achieve that?' and write down all the answers."

Bell

"Now let's all gather round the first person with their picture, and allow that person to tell us about the achievement and their qualities.

"Does anyone want to suggest any other qualities – evident from what we've just heard – that the person might like to add to the list?"

Continue round the group in turn.

Equipment

- Flip chart or poster paper.

- Drawing materials – preferably bold, colourful felt-tips or similar.

Debrief

- "How many of these resources is the team/organisation tapping into?"

- "Given these resources, what are these people capable of achieving?"

26. Shields and Crests

Participants	Time	Energy Level	Individual	Team	Visual	Verbal	Physical
4 - 12	40 Minutes	★	★ ★ ★ ★	★	★ ★ ★ ★ ★	★	★

This can be a productive way for a group to reflect on, note and share information about their resources. Participants often like to keep their handiwork long after the event.

Trainer says:

You have twenty minutes to design and draw a shield or crest that represents you. Divide it into four sections, to depict:

- an achievement

- a talent

- a personal quality

- an ambition

"You can use realistic images if you like, or if you prefer you can use symbols as in heraldry."

Bell

Now each person presents and explains their shield to the group.

Debrief

- "What did you discover about yourself during that activity?"

- "What surprised you about the others in the group?"

Equipment

- Paper

- Pens

27. Vanishing Box

Participants	Time	Energy Level	Individual	Team	Visual	Verbal	Physical
5 - 30	5 Minutes	★	★ ★ ★ ★ ★			★ ★ ★ ★	★ ★

A useful activity if you suspect that participants have concerns or cares that they would like to put aside. Also useful immediately before any creative activity, to set aside (typically) fears and inhibitions, thus opening the door to spontancity and improvisation.

Trainer says:

"I'm walking round now with a Vanishing Box, into which you may each throw one concern or attitude or anything else that you would prefer to do without for the rest of this event.

"As it's a mimed Vanishing Box, it can't take anything physical, though I could make an exception for your wallets.

"You may either state what it is as you throw it in, or simply contribute silently so that only you know what you've dumped.

"When I've finished going round the group, we shall take a vote on whether to lock the box, or destroy it by a means of your choice. If we simply lock it, you may have your items back at the end of the event if you would like to do so."

Variations/developments

With some groups, it makes more sense for the facilitator to decide whether or not the items placed in the Vanishing Box should be named aloud or not.

Debrief

Ask near the end of the event:

- "Did the things stay in the box?"

- "Would you like them back now?"

28. Time to Connect

Participants	Time	Energy Level	Individual	Team	Visual	Verbal	Physical
2 - 100	35 Minutes	★ ★	★ ★ ★ ★	★	★ ★ ★ ★ ★	★	★

This activity makes the idea of a historical timeline personal. We end up with a visual representation of significant events and resources.

Trainer says:

"Take a long sheet of paper and map out a timeline of your most important events regarding whatever it is we are dealing with during this programme.

"Each node on the timeline should have a date and either a written or drawn reminder of the event that took place at that time."

Sidecoach

• "It's OK to project your timeline into the future and predict events that you intend to happen but which haven't happened yet."

• "What other events are relevant?"

Variations/developments

Specify how many events you want on the timeline.

You can ask for individual or group timelines.

Drawing can be on a wall, tabletop or floor.

Insist that each event be depicted visually.

Debrief

- "What resources did you need to achieve these mileposts?"

- "What does the distribution through time tell you about your resources for your current challenges?"

 Equipment

Plenty of paper and coloured pens.

Emotions and Attitudes

29. Peepholes

Participants	Time	Energy Level	Individual	Team	Visual	Verbal	Physical
6 - 100	5 Minutes	★ ★	★ ★ ★	★ ★	★ ★ ★ ★		★ ★

A good warm-up activity for any session in which you plan to deal explicitly with emotions, as this offers each participant the choice of the degree to which they wish to reveal themselves.

Trainer says:

"Wander around the room in any directions you want to go. Hold your hands over your eyes, so that you are just peeping out – with enough vision for your own safety.

"Imagine your hands are like barn doors, and you can open them as wide as you like, for as long or short a time as you like, in order to reveal your face to anyone in your immediate field of vision. Reveal only as much as feels comfortable."

Sidecoach

• "Don't walk round in a circle. Vary the direction so that you get to meet plenty of people."

• "Start with quick flashes. Then show some more, when you feel it's appropriate."

Debrief

• "What are the influences on how safe you feel?"

- "Did you feel able to open up to some people more than others? What makes it different from one person to another?"

- "Why are the eyes called 'the window of the soul'?"

Impro note

This activity gives a very clear sense of freedom – namely the choice of how "open" the peepholes will be – within a simple structure. As participants feel more comfortable, so they become more expressive and willing to reveal themselves.

30. Pass the Expression

Participants	Time	Energy Level	Individual	Team	Visual	Verbal	Physical
5 - 15	5 Minutes	★ ★	★ ★	★ ★ ★	★ ★ ★ ★		★ ★

An activity played in a circle, as a kind of visual Chinese Whispers.

Trainer says:

"A volunteer, please, to make a facial expression – perhaps happiness or sadness or some other emotion. Now, holding that expression, turn to the person on your left. Person on the left, copy the expression as exactly as you can, and swing round to *your* left, and pass the expression on to the next person.

"Once you've passed it on, you can keep it or relax it, as you prefer.

"At the end of the round, the person to the left of the original volunteer starts a new expression, which is also passed round the whole group. And so on, until everyone has launched one expression – or more."

Sidecoach

• "Increase the speed."

• "Decrease the speed."

Debrief

• "What changes, if any, did changing your expression make to your emotional state?"

• "Could you identify the emotion conveyed by the expressions that the person to your right was making?"

Development

Add a gesture to the expression and pass that round the circle. Then add a posture.

31. Sculpt In Emotion

Participants	Time	Energy Level	Individual	Team	Visual	Verbal	Physical
8 - 80	20 Minutes	★ ★ ★ ★	★ ★ ★	★ ★	★ ★ ★	★ ★	★ ★ ★

A gentle way of introducing:

- Emotion

- Physical involvement – in the form of a very easy mime

- Improvisation – with an unchanging structure and just a taste of freedom

Trainer says:

"First we're going to list as many emotions as we can think of to fill this page of the flipchart. Please call them out …"

Sidecoach

It's better to have a good variety of emotions to work with for this activity, so you could ask from time to time for "a contrasting emotion" or "some more positive emotions".

I find it is fine to accept suggestions that are not-exactly-emotions, such as "drunkenness" or "dead", which sometimes get called out.

Trainer says:

"Now divide into two groups. Group A is the first performing group, and group B is the audience. We'll swap round in about five minutes.

"Everyone in Group A find a space where you can pretend to paint a portrait or make a sculpture of one of the members of Group B.

"Begin your painting or sculpture – in mime – now. The complete work is going to take about five minutes, so take your time, and concentrate on the details: brushes, clay, positioning of the canvas, and so forth.

"Continue to work, and also listen as I talk to Group B. Group B – you're going to send Group A on an emotional journey, by suggesting emotions from our list that can inform their work. We'll give them one emotion at a time, which they will feel as they do their work, and we may or may not see what effect that has.

"Group A, your job as you continue the painting or sculpture is to feel the emotion, as genuinely as you can. It doesn't matter how you happen to express it – let's just see what happens.

"Group B, first emotion, please.

"And now another emotion …"

Development

Run the activity again, asking participants to experiment with slow transitions and instant transitions between emotions.

Debrief

• "How easy was it for you to genuinely feel each of the emotions?"

• "Which transitions were easy for you? Which difficult?"

• "As spectator, how much difference did each emotion have on the way the performers expressed themselves?"

• "As performer, how much did your expression change with each emotion, do you think?"

Equipment

Flipchart

32. Foreign Circles

Participants	Time	Energy Level	Individual	Team	Visual	Verbal	Physical
5 - 12	20 Minutes	★ ★	★ ★	★ ★ ★	★ ★	★ ★ ★	★

A storytelling circle activity that encourages the speaking of meaningful nonsense – in order to illuminate some of the essences of communication. And have some fun.

Trainer says:

"Between us we're going to tell a story in a made-up foreign language – and translate it as we go along. The first person begins the story with one sentence in a made-up foreign language. The next person in the circle offers an instant translation of that sentence.

"Clearly, you'll be improvising here as there is no such language as the one we are listening to, so you'll just have to make something up inspired by whatever it is that the first person has said.

"Now the third person gives us the next sentence in the foreign language. And the fourth person translates that. And so on, round the circle, until the story is complete."

If there is an even number in the group, the trainer can join in, so that each person alternates in each round of the circle between "foreign" and "English" speaking.

Sidecoach

- " 'Foreigners', please include words or syllables that sound a bit like English words."

- "We need more than a series of grunts – this is a language you are speaking."

- "Only one sentence at a time please."

- " 'Translators', match the length of the translation to the length of the foreign sentence."

- "Be guided by the sounds of the foreign words to find the appropriate English words."

 Debrief

- " Who created the meaning of each pair (foreign and translation) of statements?"

- "What can the 'foreigners' do to make the translators' job as easy as possible?"

- "How can we improve the storytelling element within this activity?"

33. Intensity Statements

Participants	Time	Energy Level	Individual	Team	Visual	Verbal	Physical
3 - 15	20 Minutes	★ ★	★ ★ ★ ★	★	★	★ ★ ★ ★	★ ★

This is an activity in which participants discover the impact of intensity of expression.

Trainer says:

"Each of you write three statements on a piece of paper. Each statement should be something that you might say during your working day.

"The first statement is to be something casual, of minimal significance – along the lines of 'Please pass the sugar' or 'I guess the printer will need some new paper soon.'

"The second statement will be of middling significance – 'I'll call the marketing manager about those figures.'

"The third statement contains something that is probably most important, perhaps, 'The chief executive wants to see you. He's been waiting half an hour and he's as angry as I've ever seen him.'"

Bell

Now each participant reads each of their statements to the group (or partner or syndicate group), in three ways – with:

1.   low intensity

2.   middle intensity

3.   high intensity

They use all three intensities for each statement, making nine readings per person.

Debrief

- "What was the effect of reading statements at the 'wrong' level of intensity? What was the effect on the speaker? What was the impact on the listeners?"

- "At which level of intensity do you generally operate?"

- "Are you equally comfortable with each level?"

- "What are the virtues of overstatement and of understatement?"

Equipment

Paper and pens.

34. Emos x 3

Participants	Time	Energy Level	Individual	Team	Visual	Verbal	Physical
3 - 12	25 Minutes	★ ★ ★ ★	★ ★ ★	★ ★	★ ★	★ ★ ★ ★	★ ★

An activity for developing an understanding of emotional expression, and finding ways of expanding the repertoire of emotional expression.

Trainer says:

"Each participant needs a line of about six to fifteen words. Perhaps a line you would use at an important moment during a client meeting.

"In turn, step forward as if you were engaged in that meeting and say the line, first with an emotion of your choice.

"Now the other participants will choose an emotion, which you use to inform the way you say the line a second time.

"And finally say the line for a third time, with another, contrasting, emotion chosen by the other participants."

Sidecoach

You can use the list from the "Sculpt In Emotion" activity to provide a supply of suggestions for emotions.

Debrief

•   "Can any emotion 'fit' any line, or are there some that will only 'play' in a limited number of ways?"

•   "How easy was it for you to access the emotions requested?"

- "How easy was it for you to express them?"

- "How can you ensure that the full range of emotions will be accessible to you during significant work encounters?"

- "What benefits could this bring?"

Impro note

Emotional intelligence is now joining mental flexibility and physical dexterity as a key executive and life skill. The improviser who is ready and willing to access a range of emotion gains a valuable edge.

35. Appreciation Chain

Participants	Time	Energy Level	Individual	Team	Visual	Verbal	Physical
6 - 21	60 Minutes	★		★ ★ ★ ★ ★	★	★ ★ ★ ★	★

An activity that runs parallel with other processes during an event or part of it, allowing everyone to express appreciation of everyone else, resulting in a document of appreciation for each participant to take away.

Trainer says:

"Write your own name on the top of a sheet of paper, and leave that sheet on a desk or table where anyone can see it during the breaks.

"During the breaks, go round to these sheets of paper and write something that you appreciate about the person named.

"You may be the first to start someone's sheet, or – most of the time – you will be adding to comments already there. You can read those and support them or start a new strand."

Sidecoach

• Remind people from time to time that the sheets are waiting to be filled.

• "Allow yourselves time to think carefully about what to say, rather than rushing to write everything at once."

• "Write something different for each person and different from whatever anyone else has written for one person."

Development

Insist that each comment is based on something observed directly during the current event.

Insist that each comment includes mention of a specific incident between the two people involved.

Debrief

- "Would anyone like to comment on what has been written on his or her appreciation sheet?"

- "Would anyone like to comment on anything they have written on the sheets?"

Scenarios

36. Silent Rooms

Participants	Time	Energy Level	Individual	Team	Visual	Verbal	Physical
8 - 24	30 Minutes	★ ★	★ ★	★ ★ ★	★ ★ ★		★ ★ ★

A quiet yet intensive activity, which draws on the imagination of participants and observers. Although the demands are quite challenging, there's a permanent escape clause that means nobody is under any pressure to explain anything.

Trainer says:

"What we're going to do is create a series of rooms or interior spaces – without using speech. There'll be things going on in these spaces – some may be odd, others obvious. And there'll be only one person in each space at any one time.

"Groups of four, five, six or seven will each perform this activity in turn, with everyone else as a spectator.

"The only decision the group is allowed to take in advance is which member of the group goes first. Everything else is improvised – decided as you go along, in the very act of doing it.

"The person who goes first is the one who begins to define the space. You do this by coming in through the entrance, wherever and whatever you decide that to be. Then you create one aspect of the space – something that's in it or an aspect of it.

"Let's suppose you've imagined it's a cathedral. As you enter, you'll look at the vast arena and will move reverentially, perhaps. You may decide you've come to pray, in which case you'll kneel and make the appropriate signs.

"Then you leave, either through the same entrance or by another exit that the imagined space offers.

"Now another member of the group enters, acknowledging (by which we mean do nothing to destroy or negate) whatever has already been established. The second person now adds something to the location. In our example, perhaps this person has come to light a candle, and mimes striking of a match and so on.

"When the second person leaves, the third enters, and so on, along the line until the scene or story is complete. By then we may have seen someone furtively steal a candlestick, a tourist take photographs, a student make a brass rubbing and a cleaner wield a broom between the pews.

"Any activity is fine, as long as it follows the improvisational principle of *Yes ... And*, in which the 'yes' means accepting whatever the previous player has put into place, and 'and' means adding something new of your own."

However, because some people are shy about miming, we don't ask anyone what it is they thought they were doing. They have their interpretation, we have ours, and it is possible they are the same.

Sidecoach

• "You can make sounds and noises, but not intelligible speech."

• "It's easier if you mime with respect to the space, without needing other (imaginary) people to be there."

• "Remember where you put the door."

• "Don't walk through the wall. The audience will notice."

• Encourage whoever goes first in subsequent groups to create a contrasting or very different interior location. Variables include size, purpose of the space, materials from which it is made.

Debrief

- "Does anyone need to say anything about what they did?"

- "Does anyone need to ask anyone what he or she did – bearing in mind they don't have to answer?"

- "What did you find challenging about that game?"

- "What did you find liberating?"

- "How much did you enjoy expressing yourself without words?"

37. Playlets: Chair, Magic and End with a Bang

Participants	Time	Energy Level	Individual	Team	Visual	Verbal	Physical
9 - 90	30 Minutes	★ ★ ★	★	★ ★ ★ ★	★ ★ ★	★ ★ ★	★ ★ ★

Here we have the challenge of creating a simple, semi-improvised scene, around a structure that provides a central idea, image or prop.

Trainer says:

"Each group has ten minutes to prepare a short playlet – of no more than three minutes – that must include the given information in a significant way.

"The first is a playlet with a chair. The next is a playlet with magic. The third playlet ends with a bang. Each group presents their playlet in turn."

Variations/developments

As described, this activity is for three groups of three to eight players. Groups could do one scene each, or all three. For more groups or more scenes, add new prompting words, such as "playlet with a sudden exit", "foreigner", "stone", "closed window", "time machine", or whatever.

A second playlet with the same title must use the object in a different way. If the chair was used as a chair in the first playlet, it must be something else – for example, turned upside down as a packing crate – in the next.

Be more specific about the message the scene is attempting to convey – for example, "The scene should illustrate two major benefits of delegation".

Debrief

- "What message did the audience gather from the playlet?"

- "Which elements were pertinent to the workplace situation?"

38. Slideshow

Participants	Time	Energy Level	Individual	Team	Visual	Verbal	Physical
4 - 40	20 Minutes	★ ★ ★ ★	★	★ ★ ★ ★	★ ★ ★	★ ★ ★	★

The activity combines a lecture or presentation by one of the participants, with improvised physical vignettes by the rest of the group (of three to ten members).

Trainer says:

"One of the group is going to give an impromptu lecture about a subject chosen by the audience. The other members of the group will be the slideshow of visuals that the lecturer chooses to display.

"Click your fingers to bring a slide on, and click again to take the slide off. When you click on, the group must form the image within ten seconds – and without discussion.

"At the next click, all slide participants clear the stage instantly.

"A slide can have depth, but remember the audience is looking front on, as if at a screen."

Sidecoach

- "Slide participants stay still. It's a slide, not a video."

- "You can be things other than people – particularly in combination."

- "Your visuals could include photographs, graphs, diagrams."

- "Try clicking for one of the slides without describing it in advance. Or be provocative: 'When I first saw my next slide I was shocked.' Click."

Debrief

*   "How were the lecturer and the slide participants able to cooperate without discussing it in advance?"

*   "How could the slide participants create the slides without discussion?"

*   "Who was the leader?"

Variations/developments

Slideshows about work topics.

Slideshows about any subject suggested by the group.

39. Catchphrases

Participants	Time	Energy Level	Individual	Team	Visual	Verbal	Physical
3 - 36	20 Minutes	★ ★	★	★ ★ ★ ★	★ ★	★ ★ ★ ★	★

The beginnings of ritual – a shared procedure that underscores teamwork. The team works together to create something itself designed to bond the team.

Trainer says:

"Each group invents a catchphrase that they think they would like to use with some frequency at work.

"Each group in turn then presents a short scene or series of scenes, featuring the catchphrase, in order to teach its meaning, purpose and potential use to the other groups."

Debrief

- "What are the characteristics of a successful catchphrase?"

- "What is their value to a group or organisation?"

Variations/developments

An easier variation is for a group to decide on a group name, slogan or well-known phrase that unites or describes them.

A riskier variation is for them to name other groups that they deal with. The risk here is of negative or inaccurate labelling, which requires discussion before the news leaks out to the victims. The benefit is that this is often a discussion worth having.

40. First Date

Participants	Time	Energy Level	Individual	Team	Visual	Verbal	Physical
6 - 18	25 Minutes	★ ★ ★	★ ★	★ ★ ★	★ ★ ★	★ ★	★ ★

Mostly for fun, for a group that is enjoying itself and wants a novel activity. These are scenes they'd like to see. For a more work-specific variant, make the dates with new customers, important clients, the next negotiator.

Trainer says:

"This is for volunteers, to play scenes that are the first date between two people of the audience's choice. One might be a member of your organisation, and the other someone famous – a character from anywhere in the world, past or present, fictional or real.

"The two volunteers take the stage, and play out the short scene together."

Variations/developments

The characters may speak only when they are in physical contact.

Play backing music to create different moods, switching moods during the scene.

Sidecoach

If the scene is faltering, ask the audience what they'd like to see happen next – and the players must respond appropriately.

Debrief

- "What did we learn about the character presented?"

- "Who else would we like to see in a scene?"

41. Before/During/After

Participants	Time	Energy Level	Individual	Team	Visual	Verbal	Physical
6 - 60	40 Minutes	★ ★	★	★ ★ ★ ★	★ ★ ★ ★	★	★

An improvisational activity that can be applied to almost any change situation. It's easy to do and often tremendously illuminating.

Trainer says:

"Each group is going to present a series of three tableaux to the others. The three tableaux are freeze-frames or stills, in turn representing the situation as it used to be, as it is now, and as you would like it to be in the future.

"The presentation is on stage, and you can use people as people or things, and you can portray people other than yourselves. We'll allow only the minimum of necessary explanation. The scene should as much as possible speak for itself.

"You have fifteen to twenty minutes to prepare your three tableaux. When you present, hold each position in turn for about thirty seconds, so we can take in all the details."

Variations/developments

Each character in the tableau is allowed to speak one line.

The past/present/future order can be varied.

Instead of "as you would like it to be in the future", for some sessions it may be preferable to say "as you expect it to be in the future".

For some situations, specify how far back in the past and how far forward in the future.

Debrief

- "What were the key messages from each of the groups you observed?"

- "Were those messages the ones you intended to convey?"

- "What has to happen for us to reach the image of the future that was presented?"

42. Transmitters

Participants	Time	Energy Level	Individual	Team	Visual	Verbal	Physical
6 - 18	30 Minutes	★ ★ ★ ★	★	★ ★ ★ ★	★ ★ ★	★ ★	★

This tests and develops ingenuity in communicating. And, if the "transmitter" doesn't succeed immediately, then it results in a search for instant creativity.

The essence of the game is for someone to leave the room, then return to guess a piece of information. This information could be one item from a list of key concepts developed during an event, a particular product, a location – whatever seems most appropriate for the event you are running.

Trainer says:

"One member of the group is going out of the room and when they return they must play a scene with the transmitter to discover the key concept that will be allocated while they are out.

"The transmitter must convey the information as subtly as possible to give the guesser a reasonable – but not too obvious – chance."

The group selects the item of information, and then invites the guesser back into the room. And the scene is played, aiming to last for about two minutes.

Sidecoach

Ask the transmitter to find a completely new approach to suggesting the information.

The setting for the scene doesn't have to have anything to do with the information being conveyed.

Debrief

• "What were the frustrations in that form of communication?"

• "How did you overcome them?"

• "How were you able to be creative when you needed a fresh way of communicating, after initial 'failure'?"

Variations/developments

If transmitter activities are defined as those when someone leaves the room and returns in order to discover information, then there are many transmitter variations.

Some of the variants include:

• The players are not allowed to use proper language, and may speak only gibberish.

• There's a longer chain of transmitters. A passes information to B, who passes it to C.

• The transmitter must convey three pieces of information during a scene.

• Other players can come in to help the transmitter or receiver.

Creativity

43. Symbolic Name Badge

Participants	Time	Energy Level	Individual	Team	Visual	Verbal	Physical
2 - 100	10 Minutes	★ ★	★ ★ ★ ★	★	★ ★ ★ ★ ★	★	★

A neat alternative to standardised name badges at the start of a meeting or event.

Trainer says:

"As you get ready for today's events, please make yourself a name badge from the materials provided. The badge should include your name, and also a symbol that you feel represents you in some way."

Bell

"Now please each introduce yourself to the group, show us your symbol and – if you like – say what it means to you or why you have chosen it to represent you."

Variations/developments

People introduce themselves to each other one at a time in a series of pairs. This can be less intimidating and more friendly, but can also take a little more time.

It also opens up the possibility – which can be an instruction – to offer a different explanation of the symbol to each person they meet. Which is a more elaborate exercise in creativity and imagination.

Debrief

• "What did you learn about yourself?"

- "What did you learn about others in the group?"

- "What did you learn about creativity?"

44. Gift-boxes

Participants	Time	Energy Level	Individual	Team	Visual	Verbal	Physical
4 - 100	15 Minutes	★ ★ ★ ★	★ ★ ★ ★	★	★ ★	★ ★ ★	★ ★

A simple structure for imaginative improvisation, which generally surprises participants with the amount they are able to achieve.

Trainer says:

"Find a partner. One of you holds a giant imaginary gift box, which is capable of containing all the gifts on earth – and beyond. Offer the box to your partner.

"Your partner is to mime pulling gifts out of the box, naming each one as it emerges. Once it's named, throw it away and pull out another. You can do this as fast as you like. When it starts to flow, you can become very spontaneous. You'll just get a sense very quickly of what each item is. And it can be anything.

"The role of the person holding the gift box is simply to encourage your partner, saying 'Yes, so it is' and prompting only if your partner dries up. Permissible prompts include 'And what's that over there?' and category prompts, such as 'something large', 'something valuable' or 'something from France …'"

Bell

"After about three minutes, swap roles, with the partner now holding the box."

Sidecoach

"Keep going. There's plenty more in there. Look, there's something from the garden ..."

Debrief

• "Who was surprised by the amazing powers of their imagination?"

• "How did you think of all those things?"

• "How useful were the prompts and encouragements?"

Variations/developments

Play a second round, with either the same or new partners. There's really no limit to how many different objects people will find. At some point, participants may start to wonder about rules, such as whether or not they are "allowed" repetition. It can be fun to say that they are and question why they might have thought otherwise. Creativity and originality enjoy an unusual relationship.

45. Statues

Participants	Time	Energy Level	Individual	Team	Visual	Verbal	Physical
4 - 20	15 Minutes	★ ★ ★	★ ★ ★	★ ★	★ ★ ★ ★		★ ★

A quick-fire activity to prompt the imagination and get people moving.

Trainer says:

"One volunteer steps into the middle and adopts a pose – any pose. This pose is then held still like a statue.

"Other participants come up quickly one at a time and say or do something that makes sense of the statue.

"For example, the volunteer may stand with one hand out, palm upwards. First participant walks up and says, 'Yes, it's just started raining.' The next mimes putting a coin in the hand, saying, 'That's the loveliest piece of busking I've ever heard.'

"When inspiration flags, the first statue retires and someone else adopts a new pose."

Sidecoach

* "Step into the scene with the statue even if you don't know what you are going to do. Something will occur to you spontaneously."

* "You may have a second turn, if you have another idea. Otherwise, someone else form a statue."

* "Treat the statue as a thing rather than a person, if that helps."

Variations/developments

Two people form a statue together.

Debrief

- "Where do the ideas come from?"

- "What helps you to be creative?"

- "How does the pressure of entering a scene without a preformed idea work for you?"

46. Fish, Cable, Catapult

Participants	Time	Energy Level	Individual	Team	Visual	Verbal	Physical
3 - 12	25 Minutes	★	★ ★ ★ ★ ★		★	★ ★ ★ ★	★ ★

A storytelling activity that is a good stretch for beginners to improvisation. It can teach a fair bit about the craft of storytelling, as well as indicating the need for concentration, while warning of the dangers of too much ambition.

 Trainer says:

"We're going to form a storytelling circle. When it's your turn to tell a story, you'll be given three suggestions from the rest of the group. You have to incorporate these three things into the story that you tell. How you do it, the nature and length of the story is entirely up to you."

 Sidecoach

"It usually helps to repeat your three items a couple of times before you begin the story."

 Debrief

- "Who knew the whole shape of the story before they started telling it?"

- "Who worked from one item to the next to the third and hoped the story would somehow work itself out?"

- "Which is the best approach?"

- "What do you know about story craft?"

- "How ambitious does it pay to be in telling these types of story?"

47. Metaphors

Participants	Time	Energy Level	Individual	Team	Visual	Verbal	Physical
3 - 18	15 Minutes	★ ★	★ ★ ★ ★	★	★	★ ★ ★ ★	

A circle activity for encouraging creativity and revealing the nature of metaphor, a powerful way of viewing issues and problems.

Trainer says:

"The first person says a concept – such as life, families, education.

"The second person says an object, a noun, such as a shoe, a sandwich or cassette tape.

"The third person says, 'First thing is like the second thing: it's …'

"For example:

- 'Life is like a shoe: people are always walking over you'

- 'Life is like a shoe: you're always growing out of it.'

- 'Families are like sandwiches: you quickly have your fill.'

- 'Education is like a cassette tape: the good bits are worth listening to more than once.'"

Sidecoach

For the first person: "Think of a big word. Capital-letter words."

For second person: "Think of a small word. A thing. Something specific. Don't make the link with the first word – that's not your job. Be random."

For third person: "Say the first idea that comes into your head. Anything will do. There's no pressure to be good or clever."

Variation

This can be played by a large group in a circle, which involves more pressure and is often entertaining; or by smaller groups, with less pressure and more turns for each participant.

Debrief

•   "How did you deal with the pressure to be creative – particularly when it was your turn to make the link?"

•   "Which metaphors have we generated so far that could be useful to us in our work setting?"

Development

Play a further round in which the metaphors are pointed towards work situations: "An office is like …"; "Working hard is like …"; "The new change programme is like …"

48. Instant Playwrights

Participants	Time	Energy Level	Individual	Team	Visual	Verbal	Physical
2 - 50	50 Minutes	★★	★★	★★★	★★	★★★	★★

An activity that makes the participants seem tremendously creative, and leads easily from writing to performing and from working in a pair to presenting to the whole group.

Trainer says:

"You're going to write a short play in pairs. A writes the first line, and says it aloud to B. B writes the response and says it aloud to A.

"A writes the next response and the routine continues until you agree that you have reached the end of the scene. Other than this, there is no discussion.

"Each play is a maximum of sixteen lines."

Sidecoach

• "The only voices we hear should be reading out a line from your play. No other discussion. Direct any questions about the process to the facilitator."

• "You may recap by rereading the script from the top to recapture the flow."

• "You can each have a copy of your script, or you can just write your own lines – whichever is going to be easier for the forthcoming performance."

Bell

Now each pair performs their play to the other pairs.

 Variations/developments

Particularly for beginners, the facilitator dictates the first line of the play. This also illustrates the range of possibilities even when everyone shares a departure point.

Possible first lines include:

- "The equipment's ready. Let's begin."

- "I've never seen you in this mood before."

- "Hold this for me please while I unscrew the top."

 Debrief

- "How much better would the plays have been if you had been allowed to discuss the lines?"

- "What are the lessons of working this way?"

49. Die

Participants	Time	Energy Level	Individual	Team	Visual	Verbal	Physical
4 - 16	30 Minutes	★ ★ ★	★ ★ ★	★ ★		★ ★ ★	★ ★

In this storytelling activity, the emphasis is keeping the story – and the participants – alive, while under the pressure of a call of "Die". From four to eight storytellers at a time is a manageable size. The larger the audience, the greater the pressure to perform.

Trainer says:

"In the story you are about to tell, if anyone hesitates or says 'um' or repeats what has already been said, the observers/audience will shout 'Die!' – and that person drops out from this round. The winner is the last person to carry on with fluent storytelling.

"The pointer will point to whoever's telling the story at any given moment. Speak when you're pointed at, stop speaking when the pointer's finger moves on to another participant.

"The title of the story will be a character suggested by one member of the group, and a household object suggested by another. For example, 'Admiral Nelson and the lamp stand' or 'Bill Gates and the comfy chair'.

"Each time a teller dies, we'll start a new chapter of that story. Remember to keep moving the story on, particularly from chapter to chapter."

Sidecoach

Practice the shout of "Die!" on the count of three, once or preferably twice before the start, to loosen inhibitions.

The pointer can vary the speed of transitions from one teller to another. This unpredictability makes it far more interesting for participants and audience.

Use the pointing to keep the story flowing, by moving on at the right moment, and bringing in the storyteller, who will move it on helpfully at that point.

If a storyteller is flagging, prompt the audience to shout "Die!" – "No mercy".

Debrief

- "How did the pressure to perform affect the creativity required to tell the story?"

- "How can you improve your storytelling performance – individually and collectively?"

- "How clear was the communication between pointer and the tellers, and how did that affect the flow of the story?"

Impro note

To perform well requires a great mixture of listening skills, alertness and readiness, plus a willingness to commit when it's your turn.

50. Four-Line Scenes

Participants	Time	Energy Level	Individual	Team	Visual	Verbal	Physical
4 - 20	25 Minutes	★ ★	★ ★ ★	★ ★	★	★ ★	★ ★ ★

This is a transitional step into full, dramatic improvisation. Participants present scenes whose only limits are that they contain just two players, and they must speak precisely four lines of dialogue. It is a structure that clearly offers a lot of freedom, and is therefore one of the most advanced and challenging activities in the book.

Trainer says:

"You're going to create some short scenes, each of which represents one of the processes you use at work – for example, one scene might be 'Dealing with an angry customer', another might be 'How to ask for a meeting with the chief executive', a third could be 'closing a sale'.

"Each scene consists of two players, speaking precisely four lines of dialogue between them. You'll find that gives you enough for the real heart of a scene, with a beginning, middle and end.

"Two minutes to prepare each scene."

Variations/developments

Allow no preparation time.

Ask the group to generate a list of scene titles in advance on a flipchart and allow pairs to decide which scenes they will offer.

Scenes do not have titles, but each represents a plausible meeting between the two people who create the scene. Call up any two people and ask them to improvise a typical encounter they might have – and to do it in four lines only.

Debrief

- "Discuss what is working well with each of the processes illustrated."

- "What could we do better in these processes?"

- "Play revised four-line scenes, incorporating the new suggestions."

Wisdom

51. Intuition

Participants	Time	Energy Level	Individual	Team	Visual	Verbal	Physical
3 - 99	10 Minutes	★ ★	★	★ ★ ★ ★	★ ★ ★	★ ★	★

A good introductory activity, particularly when there are several people who do not know each other. It is low-energy, but intensive, and opens up routes towards many interesting interpersonal connections.

Trainer says:

"You're all endowed with the gift of intuition, and here's your chance to practise it. You will each say three things to a partner – and your partner will say three things to you. You can either say all three in quick succession or alternate.

"The first is to say 'It's obvious ...', completing the sentence with something that is obvious to you about your partner. For example, 'It's obvious you have a tattoo on your left hand.'

"The second is to say 'I notice ...', completing with something you notice about your partner. For example, 'I notice you are wearing a wig' or 'I notice your foot is tapping.'

"The third is the intuitive statement, which goes, 'My intuition tells me ...' or, if you prefer, 'I guess ...'.

"And you might say, 'My intuition tells me you have three children.'

"At the end of the sequence, your partner will tell you how accurate you have been."

The most remarkable intuitions sometimes emerge: one man told his partner "I guess you like insects", only to discover that he did indeed have a collection of stick insects.

Variations/developments

Groups of three, with A speaking to B, B to C and C to A, works well too.

After debriefing, many groups enjoy playing a second round, perhaps with new partners.

Debrief

- "How accurate were your intuitions?"

- "What interesting things did we find out about each other?"

- "How did you react when your intuitions were wrong?"

- "What's the role of intuition in business?"

52. Slow-mo

Participants	Time	Energy Level	Individual	Team	Visual	Verbal	Physical
4 - 20	30 Minutes	★ ★ ★	★	★ ★ ★ ★	★ ★ ★	★	★ ★ ★

Key moments are embedded into scenes and slowed down for portrayal and examination in detail.

This activity works for important moments in any process – such as the movements required to handle materials, or the body language, gestures and facial expressions that should greet a prospective customer.

 Trainer says:

"Let's make a list of the most critical moments of your work processes that we are dealing with during this event.

"Now some of you are going to play a short scene, in the middle of which the key moment of one of these is going to feature.

"The scene starts thirty seconds before that moment, and after half a minute you play the moment concerned in slow motion, so we can see every movement, nuance and gesture in detail."

 Sidecoach

- "I'm hitting the slow-mo button now."

- "Go back to normal speed."

- "This bit isn't crucial, so let's do it in fast-forward, with jerky movements and squeaky voices."

Debrief

- "What did we notice?"

- "Which elements were most important?"

- "How could they be improved?"

 Development

Replay the scenes in the light of the debriefing discussion.

Either the same players go again, or switch to allow others a turn.

53. Split-Screen Interview

Participants	Time	Energy Level	Individual	Team	Visual	Verbal	Physical
2 - 12	50 Minutes	★	★ ★ ★ ★ ★		★ ★ ★	★ ★	★

Using one video camera and one monitor screen, each participant conducts a conversation with him- or herself. It can be an interview, an appraisal, or two completely different sides of that person's character.

Trainer says:

"Prepare a set of questions that one of your 'characters' is going to ask your other 'character'.

"We now record these questions, with the camera shooting a close-up of the face, and the face looking about thirty degrees to one side.

"Pause between questions or (more challengingly) leave exactly as much time for tape to run through as you estimate the answer will take.

"Now sit the participant next to the monitor and play back the question tape through it.

"The camera shoots as tightly as possible to capture the monitor and the second 'character'.

"The second character answers the questions posed by the first character.

"Now play back the complete interview."

Debrief

- "What did you think of your interviewing skills – as questioner, as respondent?"

133

- "How much difference will having a live and responsive questioner make?"

Development

Play the same set of questions two or three times and change the style of your responses each time.

Notice the differences in playback. This is particularly effective if the "interviewer" is fairly neutral.

Each subsequent participant will learn a lot from their predecessors, if you allow them to observe. They'll discover, for example, the importance of the interviewer's appearing to react to the answers.

Equipment

Video camera, monitor and leads.

54. What You Should Have Said ...

Participants	Time	Energy Level	Individual	Team	Visual	Verbal	Physical
8 - 100	40 Minutes	★ ★ ★	★ ★	★ ★ ★	★ ★	★ ★ ★	★

The French call it "coup d'escalier" – the witty blow (*coup*) you wish you had uttered but that strikes you only afterwards, as you make your way down the stairs (*l'escalier*). With this activity, you get a chance to make an instant replay not only of what you should have said, but also what you think your colleagues should have said.

Trainer says:

"A number of you will play a scene regarding some aspect of the organisation's activities, and, at any point during the scene, any member of the audience may shout 'Freeze'.

"The action stops, and the person who called 'Freeze' will suggest the line that they wanted to hear. We'll wind the scene back, incorporate the new suggestion and discover what difference it makes."

Sidecoach

• "Are you sure that was the best way of handling that point?"

• "Shout 'Freeze' if you think the response was unrealistic."

Debrief

• "What lessons can we take forward into the organisation?"

• "How shall we do things differently from now on?"

During the debrief, discuss as little as possible. If any of the points raised can be fed into the scene, put them into action in a scene and *observe* the impacts.

55. Consult Your Consultant

Participants	Time	Energy Level	Individual	Team	Visual	Verbal	Physical
1 - 100	25 Minutes	★	★ ★ ★ ★	★	★ ★	★ ★ ★ ★	★

Derived from the practices of solution-focused brief therapy, this invites participants to access their own wisdom.

Trainer says:

"On your own, take the problem or most critical issue that currently faces you. Now imagine you are a wise, experienced and sympathetic consultant who you have brought in at a vast fee to advise about this issue.

"What does the consultant say to you?"

Variations/developments

For issues that are more personal than professional, suggest that they imagine that the "consultant" is their older, wiser self, and that they are looking back helpfully to this earlier issue or crisis in their lives. They know how it worked out – and it worked out well, we should assume – and it's from this perspective that the "advice" is proffered.

Debrief

* "What good suggestions did you make?"

* "Where do you usually keep all that wisdom?"

* "How can you access it more often?"

Impro note

It is amazing how easily people can make this kind of imaginative leap. Creativity does not need to be mystical or difficult. A useful note at the beginning of any session involving improvisation is "imagine you are imaginative".

56. Telepathy

Participants	Time	Energy Level	Individual	Team	Visual	Verbal	Physical
4 - 20	10 Minutes	★ ★		★ ★ ★ ★ ★	★ ★ ★ ★	★	

A quiet activity that provides a good measure of group alignment – or otherwise. Can be used to contrast the beginning and the end of an event.

Trainer says:

"Together we're going to count from one to twenty. Anyone can say the next number in the sequence, but, if two people speak at the same time, we start again from one."

Sidecoach

• "No individual can count more than one consecutive number."

• "No discussion during the game to come up with strategies."

Debrief

• "How did you do that?"

• "How did you deal with the frustrations of failed attempts?"

• "How did the group learn from failure to turn it to success?"

• "If a leader emerged, how could the group achieve the task without the leader or without leadership?"

Variations/developments

Count from one to twenty-five.

Arrange the positioning so that not everyone can make eye contact with every-one else.

57. Absolute Zero

Participants	Time	Energy Level	Individual	Team	Visual	Verbal	Physical
4 - 30	15 Minutes	★ ★	★ ★ ★ ★	★		★ ★ ★ ★	★

A way of ending that taps into creative, improvisational resources, while summarising the day's learning (or activities). It's a participant-centred way of finishing, and allows individual scope for expression. It usually results in some amusement when participants read out their efforts.

Trainer says:

"Find yourself a partner with whom you would like to summarise the day's learning.

"Starting with the letter 'A' and finishing with 'Z', write one sentence starting with each letter of the alphabet to record what you've learned during this event."

Bell

"Now take turns to read your A to Z to the group."

Debrief

• "Any difficulties?"

• "Anything else you'd like to have said?"

Variations/developments

Do this individually (perhaps for a writing skills or individual creativity event) or in larger groups.

Equipment

Paper and pens.

Conclusion

58. Taking a bow to riotous applause

Participants	Time	Energy Level	Individual	Team	Visual	Verbal	Physical
5 - 21	5 Minutes	★ ★ ★ ★ ★		★ ★ ★ ★ ★	★	★	★ ★ ★ ★

A great finisher after any sequence of improvisational activities, leaving everyone feeling acknowledged and energised.

 Trainer says:

"With a subtle combination of great energy and astonishing dignity, each of you is going to step forward in turn and take a bow to riotous applause."

 Sidecoach

- "Let's hear it – more gusto."

- "Enjoy it – don't milk it!"

 Debrief

"How often does that happen?"

58½. Finding and devising new activities

"What's this half an activity?" people have been asking me as I prepared the book. Well, that is a good question.

Here is half an activity: use the improvisational skills you have learned so far to devise a new activity that will suit the particular needs of the participants during your next session.

Another half is this: follow the signpost to a host of further activities – another activity, if you like, of finding more activities. One place to find them (and you may consider this a shameless plug) is in the companion book, *Impro Learning – How to Make Your Training Creative, Flexible and Spontaneous*, also available in paperback as *The Inspirational Trainer* (Kogan Page).

In *Impro Learning / The Inspirational Trainer* you will find several more activities, explained in detail, placed into the contexts of designing and delivering effective learning experiences and all partaking of the improvisational flavour that I trust is apparent in this book.

You will learn how to run effective training from the planning stage to the debriefing, with many useful activities to bring out the best in learners. You will also discover when best to run them and how each brings out one or more of the principles of improvisational learning.

Bibliography

Fluegelman, Andrew (ed.), 1976, *The New Games Book*, Doubleday/Dolphin.

Jackson, Paul Z, 1998, *Impro Learning: How To Make Your Training Creative, Flexible and Spontaneous*, Gower, Aldershot.

Jackson, Paul Z, 2001, *The Inspirational Trainer* (paperback edition of *Impro Learning*), Kogan Page, London.

Jackson, Paul Z and McKergow, Mark, 2002, *The Solutions Focus*, Nicholas Brealey, London.

Rohnke, Karl, 1984, *Silver Bullets*, Kendall/Hunt, Iowa.

Scheele, Paul R., 1997, *Natural Brilliance*, Learning Strategies Corporation, Minnesota.

Scheele, Paul R., 1993, *The Photoreading Whole Mind System,* Learning Strategies Corporation, Minnesota.

USA & Canada *orders to:*
Crown House Publishing
P.O. Box 2223, Williston, VT 05495-2223, USA
Tel: 877-925-1213, Fax: 802-864-7626
www.CHPUS.com

UK & Rest of World *orders to:*
The Anglo American Book Company Ltd.
Crown Buildings, Bancyfelin, Carmarthen, Wales SA33 5ND
Tel: +44 (0)1267 211880/211886, Fax: +44 (0)1267 211882
E-mail: books@anglo-american.co.uk
www.anglo-american.co.uk

Australasia *orders to:*
Footprint Books Pty Ltd.
Unit 4/92A Mona Vale Road, Mona Vale NSW 2103, Australia
Tel: +61 (0) 2 9997 3973, Fax: +61 (0) 2 9997 3185
E-mail: info@footprint.com.au
www.footprint.com.au

Singapore *orders to:*
Publishers Marketing Services Pte Ltd.
10-C Jalan Ampas #07-01
Ho Seng Lee Flatted Warehouse, Singapore 329513
Tel: +65 6256 5166, Fax: +65 6253 0008
E-mail: info@pms.com.sg
www.pms.com.sg

Malaysia *orders to:*
Publishers Marketing Services Pte Ltd
Unit 509, Block E, Phileo Damansara 1, Jalan 16/11
46350 Petaling Jaya, Selangor, Malaysia
Tel : 03 7955 3588, Fax : 03 7955 3017
E-mail: pmsmal@po.jaring.my

South Africa *orders to:*
Everybody's Books
Box 201321 Durban North 401, 1 Highdale Road,
25 Glen Park, Glen Anil 4051, KwaZulu NATAL, South Africa
Tel: +27 (0) 31 569 2229, Fax: +27 (0) 31 569 2234
E-mail: ebbooks@iafrica.com